Len Bug and Jen Slug

Written and Illustrated
by Shelley Davidow

Jalmar Press

ISBN: 978-1-931061-46-9

Jalmar Press
PO Box 370
Fawnskin, CA 92333
(800) 429-1192
F: (909) 86-2961
www.jalmarpress.com

About the Author and Illustrator: Shelley Davidow is originally from South Africa. Her young adult book, *In the Shadow of Inyangani*, was nominated for the first African Writer's Prize by Macmillan/Picador and BBC World. The author of numerous books, Shelley lives in Florida (USA), where she is a class teacher at the Sarasota Waldorf School.

About the Readers: These early readers are phonetically based and contain stories that young children will find enjoyable and entertaining. Each story has a beginning, middle and an ending. The stories are gently humorous while honoring nature, animals and the environment.

The six books use simple words that the early reader will easily grasp. They have been carefully chosen by a reading specialist to help students advance from the short vowels, to the silent "e", to the vowel combinations. At the back of this book is a list of sight words that should be reviewed with the child before reading the book.

About our Reading Specialist: Mary Spotts has been a remedial reading teacher for over ten years, taking countless classes and seminars to keep current in the field she loves. Her deep understanding that struggling readers need good stories — particularly if the books are phonetically based — has been an inspiration in the creation of these books. Mary has been a constant guide, ensuring that the books address specific phonetic principles while retaining a gently humorous story line.

Mary's desire to have available meaningful children's stories with decodable words and Shelley's creative talents and love of literature have been the incentive and encouragement to bring these books to production.

For Emory

Len was a bug.

His hut was a nut.

He hid in his hut for days,
for the sun was hot.

Len Bug and Jen Slu

Jen was a slug.
She had no hut.

Jen got hot in the sun,
and she got wet in the rain.

Len Bug met
Jen Slug in the mud.

They slid in the mud
and sat in the sun.

Then Len Bug and Jen Slug
went to Len's nut hut.

Len Bug had a fun hut.
Jen Slug got a fun hat.
Len and Jen had fun in
the hat on Len's hut.

Then, in the sun,
Jen saw a nut.

Jen got the new nut
for her hut.

Len went to Jen's hut
in a fun hat.

Len and Jen had fun
in hats at Jen's hut.

Jen did not get wet in the rain,
and she did not get hot in the sun.

Len and Jen, a bug and a slug,
sat in fun hats on nut huts.

Short Vowel Sounds

a	e	i	o	u
at	met	in	hot	nut
hats	Jen's	hid		huts
	Len's	slid		fun
				bug
				slug

Sight Words

for

days

the

she

no

rain

new

her

CPSIA information can be obtained
at www.ICGtesting.com
Printed in the USA
BVHW081916191120
593684BV00005B/45

9 781931 061469